WELCOME TO THE NATURAL H͟ ͟ ͟UR

This booklet will help you enjoy and remember your trip in one of our count͟ ͟ ͟treasured public
lands. Remember that your driver, as an interpretive naturalist, has more complete knowledge of
Denali National Park and Preserve than can be presented in these few pages.
So ask questions, search the wilderness world
that surrounds you for what it may reveal,
and enjoy your trip!

The Weave of Wilderness

Gaze across a broad expanse of Denali National Park and Preserve, and you will see a living tapestry. Tundra carpeted with tiny wildflowers. Braided rivers. Thin-soiled slopes embroidered with the tracks of sheep and caribou.

Nature's loom never rests. Each day and every passing hour, new designs emerge, even while underlying patterns remain unchanged. Rain may freshen and brighten the colors of exposed rocks. A bear may appear, its golden hairs ruffled by the breeze. The next moment there may be only woolen fog, softening the distant, rolling hills.

What makes this living tapestry most remarkable is that it is intact.

"An ecosystem is a tapestry of species and relationships," observes nature writer David Quammen in *The Song of the Dodo*. "Chop away a section, isolate that section, and there arises the problem of unraveling."

In Denali, the weave holds. Ripening blueberries in the fall tundra provide feasts for grizzly bears and voles alike. The well-fed voles become food for wolves. Basic ecological patterns repeat undisturbed.

"AN ECOSYSTEM IS A TAPESTRY OF SPECIES AND RELATIONSHIPS. CHOP AWAY A SECTION, ISOLATE THAT SECTION, AND THERE ARISES THE PROBLEM OF UNRAVELING."

—David Quammen, *The Song of the Dodo*

Denali is a living tapestry.

► Adjust your eyes and ears to wilderness. Look and listen carefully and you may see or hear signs, like grizzly bear tracks or a bird call, that reveal the presence of the unseen.

Alaska Natives and other peoples have used this land for nearly 11,000 years, but the human footprint remains small. Despite some development in and near the park, Denali is much the same today as it has been for all those years. No rivers have been diverted here. Habitat is protected. Wolves and other animal predators continue to hunt.

The park is vast and wild: six million acres with few established trails, the largest a ribbon of road. Denali is a national treasure in part because it is a place where visitors may still see large animals at home in the wild: caribou, bear, wolf, Dall sheep, and moose. But as park pioneer Adolph Murie reminded us many years ago in *A Naturalist in Alaska*, "One need not see a wolf to benefit from his presence; it is enough to know that there is the possibility of discovering one on some distant ridge. It is enough to know that the wolf still makes his home in this beautiful wilderness region to which he contributes vividness, color and adventure . . . an emblem of unspoiled country."

Denali remains a stronghold not only for individual species but also for patterns of relationships; together these form the loom upon which true wilderness is woven. Water, soil, rock, and air. Fungi, plants, and animals both big and small. The seen and the unseen. Their connections and interactions yield a sum that is greater than its parts. In the continued weaving of its wilderness, Denali is a living masterpiece.

Interactions among animals, plants,

◄ Wildflowers bloom during the short growing season.

and elements weave a wilderness masterpiece.

5

Taiga and Tundra: Fringes and Stitches

The taiga is a quiet northern forest where plants, fungi, and animals are joined by invisible ecological threads. The treeless tundra is where Denali's living tapestry seems magical, a carpet of colors and textures that unrolls as far as the eye can see. Together, these two vegetation zones—and the fringe that runs between them—are places of struggle and adaptation, where hardship is a fact of life and quirkiness a badge of honor.

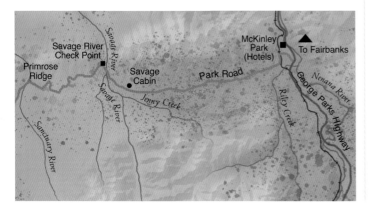

"I HAVE WALKED OVER THE GREEN, FLOWERING SLOPES IN THE RAIN, WHEN THE FOG HID THE LANDSCAPE BEYOND A FEW HUNDRED YARDS, AND FELT THAT THE WHITE MOUNTAIN AVENS, THE PURPLE RHODODENDRONS, AND THE DELICATE WHITE BELLS OF THE HEATHER AT MY FEET WERE ALONE WORTHY OF OUR EFFORTS."

—Adolph Murie, *A Naturalist in Alaska*

_____

_____

_____

_____

Northern boreal forest borders Denali.

► The knotty, rust-colored growths commonly called witches' brooms (spruce broom rust) are signs of disturbance or disease in the life of a spruce tree. However, they serve an important purpose as denning sites for tree squirrels.

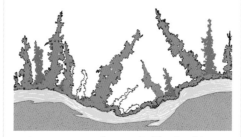

▲ A cross-sectional view of a "drunken" forest

In the park, the taiga cloaks the lower elevations, including the first dozen or so miles through which the park road passes. Beyond Denali, it is extensive, covering more than a quarter of the United States and Canada, and broad areas of Russia and Europe.

The growing season is short here: no more than 100 days. Soils are acidic, nutrients are poor, and leaf litter takes years to decompose. If not for animals such as squirrels, which consume and disperse the spores of a helpful fungi, regeneration in this northern forest would be slower yet.

Despite its vastness, the taiga is a mostly uniform place, with relatively few plant species. White spruce grow to approximately 50 feet, only a quarter of the height of spruce trees that grow farther south, in coastal Alaska. Alongside these modest evergreens grow pockets of aspen, paper birch, and balsam poplar.

Where the ground is soggy, pipecleaner-thin black spruce dominate. Many are stunted, no taller than six or seven feet, though they may have struggled for decades against wind and cold just to attain that modest height. Some "drunken" trees lean at crazy angles, their roots disturbed by the freezing and thawing of discontinuous permafrost—pockets of frozen ground—inches below the forest floor.

As the park road climbs, gaps open between the stunted trees.

Plants face extreme temperatures and a

◀ The taiga has relatively few plant species. Alongside modest evergreens grow pockets of paper birch, balsam poplar, and aspen, such as these with their autumn leaves.

_____

_____

_____

_____

_____

_____

short growing season of no more than 100 days.

 ▶ The colors of pink fireweed, purple lupine, and yellow cinquefoil brighten a hillside.

_____

_____

_____

_____

_____

_____

_____

Forested taiga yields gradually to treeless tundra at about 2,500 feet, where cold temperatures and moisture-sapping winds prevent trees from growing. The taiga gains brief footholds again where the road dips into protected valleys. This gradual transition zone—a patchwork governed by small variations in climate, soil, and topography—is a productive one for wildlife.

Bears from the treeless hills may stalk a moose calf into the forest. Raptors, like the daylight-loving hawk owl, perch atop scraggly trees at the taiga's edge, and fly toward open tundra to chase voles and mice. Like the taiga, the tundra must contend with a short growing season. It is even more exposed than taiga to abrasive, blasting winds, and plants must grow in thinner and rockier soil.

Tundra can be moist or dry. Moist tundra is brushy; what may look flat from a distance can be a nearly impenetrable, waist-high tangle of willow and birch. Dry tundra is low-lying but can still be spongy. Watch the springy step of a caribou crossing a distant ridge, and you can imagine how the tundra feels underfoot.

Tundra plants make the most of the long hours of summer daylight, as much as 20 hours out of every 24 in June. They do their best to grow during the three months in which they are not covered by snow.

Watch for movement and understand . . . the bear

◄ The treeless, rolling tundra is a great place to spot wildlife. Watch for movement, and understand, as the driver-naturalists muse, "The bear you don't see might be a bear that's never seen a human. And that's only possible in a place this large and wild."

you don't see might be a bear that's never seen a human.

Wildflowers erupt into color at summer's peak. But that floral burst comes after a long and patient wait. Many plants must grow for a decade or more before they can produce buds, and buds themselves may develop for several years before they open.

Surprisingly, in a realm this exposed, snow is not a foe but an ally; it helps to insulate tiny plants from subzero temperatures. Some evergreen plants can continue to photosynthesize—capture energy from the sun—even beneath the snow's surface.

Growing in such adverse conditions, and at such slow rates, the tundra is incredibly fragile, each shrub and flower and lichen patch a delicate stitch in Denali's tapestry.

◄ Both taiga and tundra are home to many plants used by Alaska Natives for food and medicine. Willow contains salicin, comparable to the active ingredient found in aspirin. Labrador tea (left) is used to treat colds, arthritis, and gout. Young spruce tips are high in vitamin C and can be made into tea or jelly. The inner bark of the spruce tree can be eaten as a survival food.

Many taiga plants have provided food

◄ The merlin, a small falcon, is one of several Denali raptors that nest in taiga and hunt above the alpine tundra, taking advantage of both habitats. Fierce as this bird appears, it is vulnerable to the environmental contaminants it encounters when it migrates thousands of miles south. Reproductive problems, including eggshell thinning, have been noted in Denali merlins, proving that ecological threads extend far beyond the borders of any park.

or medicine for Alaska Natives.

"PEOPLE SAY MOOSE ARE HOMELY AND AWKWARD AND SOMEWHAT ABSURD, THE PRODUCT OF SOME MISALLIANCE BETWEEN COW AND CAMEL THAT CONTRIVED THAT HUMP, THAT HERO SANDWICH OF A NOSE, THAT VAGUELY RIDICULOUS BELL DANGLING FROM THE THROAT. IN LIKENING THE PARTS OF A MOOSE TO THOSE OF OTHER ANIMALS, WE MISS THE FUNCTIONAL BEAUTY OF THE WHOLE, THE BIOLOGICAL REJOINDERS TO AN ENVIRONMENT THAT PRODUCES EVERY KIND OF HARDSHIP: SHORT SUMMERS, TERRIBLE WINTERS, NOT ENOUGH FOOD, AND A COUPLE OF THE WORLD'S MOST EARNEST PREDATORS."

—Sherry Simpson, *The Way Winter Comes*

Where tundra and taiga form a diverse mosaic, animals

◀ Taiga trees may grow slowly and with difficulty, but some taiga animals proliferate with astonishing speed. Snowshoe hare populations periodically soar, reaching densities of 600 animals per square mile, and then crash. Their main predator, the elusive lynx, responds to good hare years by giving birth to more kittens. Thus paired, the species rise and fall together, in 8- to 11-year cycles.

_____

_____

_____

_____

hunt or feed in one zone and nest or hide in another.

▲ Under a deep blanket of snow, temperatures can be much higher than in the air above the snow. Subnivean or "under-the-snow" animals such as voles take advantage of this phenomenon, tunneling their way to warmth.

▼ Butterflies in Denali? Yes, the colorful beauties live here, too, though they've adapted in many ways. In warmer climes, butterflies rest with their wings closed. On the tundra, butterflies rest with their wings open, to soak up the sun's warmth. Blue and purple are popular colors for both northern butterflies and wildflowers, because darker colors absorb heat.

The tundra is incredibly fragile, each shrub and

◄ Lichens, such as this lacy reindeer moss growing in the tundra amidst lingonberries (red) and crowberries (black), come in a variety of shapes. They can grow as colorful crusts and scaly patches so small and strange you may not realize they are living things. In fact, they're two living things in one. A fungus provides a protective surface for an alga, which in turn manufactures food for the fungus. Lichens provide more than half of the caribou's winter diet. Undisturbed, a lichen can last centuries.

flower and lichen a delicate stitch in Denali's tapestry.

Dots on a Ridge: Inspiration for the Park

Park pioneer Charles Sheldon first came to the Denali area in 1906 to hunt the Dall sheep that most often appear from the road as white dots moving on mountain ridges. A Yale-educated easterner, he sought them partly for his own trophy collection, partly as specimens for museums. Sheldon scrambled up and around mountains, across creeks, and through dense willow patches, through mist and rain, sun and wind.

At first, Sheldon's quarry eluded him. But he wasn't disappointed. There was so much more to see, from tantalizing grizzly tracks to the flash of dark eagle wings overhead. He heard the murmur of braided streams and the crash of avalanches. By the time he left, the love he felt for Denali was more important than the sheep he'd bagged.

Sheldon visited again in 1907, wintering over in a cabin on the Toklat River. The time he spent here enhanced and expanded his ideas about wilderness. With future park superintendent Harry Karstens as his

DIFFERENT USES ARE ALLOWED IN DIFFERENT AREAS OF DENALI NATIONAL PARK AND PRESERVE, BASED ON SPECIFIC PARK, PRESERVE, AND WILDERNESS DESIGNATIONS ASSIGNED BY THE UNITED STATES CONGRESS.

White Dall sheep traverse high ridges.

▶ Five years after the park's creation, the first tourist arrived. A year later, the railroad between Seward and Fairbanks was completed, enabling trains to deliver visitors to the park's doorstep in 1939 (right), just as they do today.

——————

——————

——————

——————

BY RIDING THE TOUR BUS, YOU ARE HELPING TO PROTECT DENALI'S WILDERNESS ECOSYSTEM. THE BUS PROGRAM, WHICH EMERGED IN 1972 AS AN ALTERNATIVE TO PRIVATE CAR TRAFFIC INSIDE THE PARK, MINIMIZES VISITOR IMPACTS, ALLOWING MANY TO EXPERIENCE A PARK THAT BELONGS TO US ALL WITHOUT DESTROYING IT.

guide, Sheldon trekked, mushed dogs, and recorded field notes for months. He was concerned about the numbers of sheep being slaughtered each year by commercial hunters, and imagined a refuge where both wildlife and the rhythms of this majestic land could be preserved.

Sheldon became one of several early conservationists who fought to preserve Denali. In 1917, in response to these efforts, Congress passed a bill to establish Mount McKinley National Park. Renamed Denali National Park and Preserve and expanded more than three-fold in 1980, it is now larger than the state of New Hampshire.

If Sheldon was the park's founding father, then another naturalist, Adolph Murie, was its dogged conscience. In the 1930s, biologist Adolph joined his older brother, Olaus, at the new park to study wildlife, especially wolf–sheep interactions. At the time, Denali's sheep population seemed to be in peril, and wildlife managers with less vision argued that predator control was the only option.

Adolph Murie disagreed, arguing that predators are part of what keeps an ecosystem intact and healthy. Over time, his view prevailed. Today, Denali National Park and Preserve is rare among parks for allowing populations to be self-regulating, without herd or predator management.

Murie also went on to write popular books about other

Charles Sheldon became one of several early

◄ The 91-mile park road was constructed between McKinley Park Station and Kantishna, a mining camp, from 1923 to 1938. The road made the park more accessible to visitors, and their numbers have increased steadily over the years. More than 350,000 people now visit Denali each summer.

conservationists who fought to preserve Denali.

► Harry Karstens, shown here with his dog team, was the first superintendent of the park.

► On the prowl for food, adult wolves can travel 50 miles in a day. When hunting large mammals, such as caribou, they target the weak, the old, and the sick. In this way, pioneer wildlife biologist Adolph Murie found, a predator actually strengthens, rather than destroys, its prey species.

Denali animals—of all sizes. Murie seemed to get as much joy watching a mouse gather straw or a gull wash in a puddle as he did studying wolves, bears, and caribou. Like Sheldon, Murie realized that in Denali, the fates of all creatures, great and small, are woven together.

By riding the tour bus, instead of driving, you are

◄ Dall sheep favor wind-blown ridges and steep cliff faces, where they can roam beyond the easy reach of wolves. The wild sheep rely on keen eyesight to keep track of predators.

_____

_____

_____

_____

helping to protect Denali's intricate ecosystem.

► Little has changed since Harry Karstens patrolled the park with sled dogs in the 1920s. Huskies, the park's four-footed heroes, still log about 1,000 miles each winter helping rangers conduct boundary patrols and assist visitors.

Glimpse history at cabins that are still used

◄ Strolling toward Savage Cabin, a rustic shelter just off the park road, you pass through a gateway in more ways than one. This backcountry cabin, and others like it, have been used for decades by rangers conducting winter park patrols. In summer, it serves as a living history site—a place where visitors can travel back in time and hear the words of early park advocates, staff, and settlers. The cabin also sits near the park's "designated wilderness" boundary. Beyond that boundary, land is managed to remain wild and intact.

by rangers today as they patrol the park.

Ancient Patterns of Rock and Ice

Ancient metamorphic rocks, up to a billion years old, can be seen as mountains to the north of the park road and in the canyon of the Savage River. They are part of Denali's dramatic geologic history. A half-billion years ago, the land around Denali was an ocean floor. Today it is hundreds of miles from the coast. Mixed in are geologic fragments of diverse types, dating from different eras. It is a patchwork formed through colossal movements that shape it still.

In 1980, a geologist proposed that the entire western edge of North America had been shuffled much more than previously suspected. Evidently, landmasses, called "terranes," had been carried toward Alaska by the conveyor-belt-like movement of the Pacific Plate.

This enormous plate grinds northward until it collides with the continental North American Plate. There, in the earthquake-rattled subduction zone, the Pacific Plate slides deep into the earth. But before it slides, it drops off any lighter landmasses picked up along the way. Long ago, these mismatched landmasses, reaching the end of their free ride, were scraped off and stitched onto Alaska.

"ALONE IN A WILDERNESS HUNDREDS OF MILES FROM CIVILIZATION AND HIGH ON ONE OF THE WORLD'S MOST IMPOSING MOUNTAINS, I WAS DEEPLY MOVED BY THE STUPENDOUS MASS OF THE GREAT UPHEAVAL, THE VAST EXTENT OF THE WILD AREAS BELOW, THE CHAOS OF THE UNFINISHED SURFACES STILL IN PROCESS OF MOULDING, AND BY THE CRASH AND ROAR OF THE MIGHTY AVALANCHES."

—Charles Sheldon, *The Wilderness of Denali*

A colorful geological patchwork

▶ Sedimentary rocks on Mt. McKinley's north peak began 100 million years ago as the floor of an inland sea. The mountain's granite south peak was created when molten rock rose into the sedimentary rocks about 56 million years ago. Both continue to be uplifted today by the Pacific Plate.

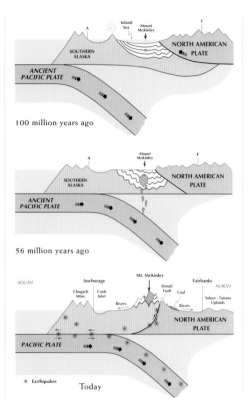

100 million years ago

56 million years ago

Today

Continued Pacific Plate movements have further buckled the terrane crazy quilt. For example, the Outer Range, which rises just north of the park road, was created by tectonic lifting about five to six million years ago. Even today, the northward pressure of the Pacific Plate lifts Mount McKinley, at 20,320 feet North America's highest peak, still higher. The creep is imperceptible, a rate of about one inch per 25 years.

The terrane theory helps explain why southern Alaska's rocks are, in the words of writer Michael Collier, in *The Geology of Denali National Park and Preserve*, "a tangled mesh of differing types of rock, interwoven faults and folds." He adds, "Rocks at Denali seem to come and go, to change from one type to another within just a few feet."

Plate tectonics are only part of what makes Denali geology so interesting. Heat and ice, in the forms of volcanoes and glaciers, have added even more patterns, colors, and shapes to the geological patchwork.

Glaciers have scraped and spilled through most of the park in successive Ice Age pulses, carving out U-shaped valleys before retreating to their high, cold birthing places. After the most recent episode, which ended less than 10,000 years ago, the largest glaciers shrank back to their icy cradles in the Alaska Range, south of the park road. There they creak, growl, and drip, feeding silty rivers that course through the park's many valleys.

The land around Denali was an ocean floor;

◄ Some of the rocks in Savage Canyon show the effects of millions of years of heat and pressure. Once ancient ocean sediments, these 400 million-year-old metamorphic rocks, called schist, were folded into chevron shapes by the forces of plate tectonics.

heat and pressure have shaped what we see today.

► The power of a single element in two very different forms—ice and water—is visible from the bridge at Savage River. Just to the south, a broad U-shaped valley, like many in Denali, was formed when an ancient glacier ground to a halt and then retreated. To the north, a V-shaped valley (right) was formed by river erosion, fed by rain, snow, and meltwater from other distant, retreated glaciers.

▲ Mining for gold, silver, lead, zinc, copper and antimony attracted settlers to the area.

Each time a channel is clogged, the river

◄ Braided rivers wander back and forth, filling only a small portion of their gravelly streambeds, even at high water. These rivers carry huge sediment loads—rocks, mud, and glacial flour—eroded by glaciers at the rivers' headwaters.

_____

_____

_____

_____

_____

_____

_____

_____

_____

changes course, adding a new ribbon to its braid.

An Ancient Thread: Athabaskans in Denali

On a blue-sky day in Denali, distance can be hard to judge. Even time may seem transparent.

Step out of the bus at Primrose Ridge, look across the broad valley that stretches all the way to the Alaska Range, and you may be standing in the historic footsteps of ancient hunters. This vast lookout was probably used by the region's first peoples.

Squint toward a tundra-carpeted ridge, and you can imagine the life of the hunter, scanning the landscape for sheep, bear, and caribou. Peer into the olive-colored shadows of the taiga, and you can understand the care taken by the gatherer, who appreciates the woodland as both pantry and pharmacy. Stand above a braided river, and you can hear the soft exchange of timeless voices, deciding where it is safest to cross.

Alaska Natives have used the Denali area for about 11,000 years, since retreat of the last great ice sheets. In fact, Denali country stands at the very heart of Athabaskan country—a place where many different groups' subsistence activities overlapped.

These Athabaskan-speaking groups included the Ahtna,

▲ Artifacts found at archaeological sites within the park reveal hunting and gathering activities that occurred 3,500 years ago.

Athabaskan heritage in Denali

Native Peoples and Languages of Alaska near Denali National Park and Preserve

ARCTIC OCEAN

Beaufort Sea

INUPIAQ

ALASKA

ATHABASKAN

Koyukon

Tanana

Upper Kuskokwim

Bering Sea

YUP'IK

Ahtna

Dena'ina

CANADA

EYAK

ALUTIQ

TLINGIT

GULF OF ALASKA

ALEUT

- ALEUT
- ALUTIQ
- ATHABASKAN
- EYAK
- INUPIAQ
- TLINGIT
- YUP'IK
- Languages in the park area (subgroups of the Athabaskans)
- Denali National Park and Preserve

Dena'ina, Upper Kuskokwim (Kolchan), Lower Tanana, and Koyukon. Although all five groups had different linguistic characteristics, they shared similar lifestyles and culture.

The harsh climate and limited resources of the subarctic interior required that Athabaskans have intimate knowledge of their environment. They traveled great distances to hunt and fish, and cooperated without regard for fixed borders. Local bands of between 20 and 75 people functioned as one economic unit. At certain times of the year, usually in winter months, regional bands, made up of several local bands related by language, met to trade and share resources, hold ceremonies, and resolve tribal matters.

Working in tandem, several bands would construct caribou fences. Hunters drove the caribou into fences and used clubs, spears, and bows and arrows to kill them.

Sharing resources was essential to survival. A "rich man" of the band usually saw to the redistribution of food to ensure that all received their share. The rich man was not a chief, as such, but a man known for his leadership qualities, good judgment, and generosity.

Today, Athabaskans and others who have traditionally used these lands continue to hunt, fish, trap, gather berries and plants, and share resources with one another. Their ongoing cultural practices form a strong thread in the fabric of the park.

Many Denali landmarks play an important part in Athabaskan oral tradition. This story is told about a remote, natural rock formation, called Geese House, to explain how the lichen-stained outcropping became streaked with black, ochre, green, yellow, and orange:

Raven was getting his feathers painted at Geese House and was being very picky about how it was done. Each time they painted him with a different color, but he was never satisfied because it wasn't bright enough. So they got mad at Raven and threw all the black paint on him. That's why he is all black.

—Julius Bettis of Nenana, as told to
Henry Ketzler, Sr., *Geese House Report*

35

Denali—The High One

The Athabaskans have their own explanations for how the landscape, including Denali, or the "High One," was shaped. Central to the sacred story is Raven.

▲ More than 1,300 mountaineers attempt to climb Mt. McKinley each year.

The Raven, incarnated as a young man, had paddled his canoe across a great body of water to ask a woman to marry him. She refused to be his wife, so he made her sink into the mud and disappear; and then he began paddling back home. The woman's mother kept two brown bears, and in her anger she told them to drown the young man. They dug furiously at the lake's edge, making huge waves everywhere on the water. But Raven calmed a narrow path before him and paddled on.

Eventually he became exhausted, so he threw a harpoon that struck the crest of a wave. At that moment he fainted from the intensity of his concentration, and when he awoke a forested land had replaced the water. He saw that the first wave his harpoon struck had become a small mountain. Then it had glanced off, eventually striking a huge wave that solidified into another mountain—the one now called Deenaalee, or Mount McKinley.

—Paraphrased from Jetté 1908:312-13, in *Make Prayers to the Raven*

Denali and Raven—two timeless spirits

Always Moving: Wildlife Through the Year

A silt-laden stream flows and shifts, carving out a wide riverbed. A caribou sniffs, paws the ground, and hurries along its way. A winter wind blows across a ridge, exposing plants and lichens that hungry caribou relish. The three make an enchanted braid: water, wind, and caribou, all colored by a northern restlessness.

In Denali, everything is moving. Wind and water, flora and fauna, all seem to be engaged in a struggle to keep pace with each other—and with the seasons, which have the most restless spirit of all.

The pikas gather grass all summer and dry it into hay. Fireweed flowers bloom and shrivel in a matter of weeks. Not long after it arrives to nest, the arctic tern must prepare to migrate back to Antarctica, a round-trip of 25,000 miles.

"Seasons tend to blow open and shut like doors in the wind up here," says driver-naturalist Aaron Coons. Even in July, it's easy to feel that winter is close at hand—as close as the permafrost a few inches below the soil, or as close as the permanent ice and snow shimmering on Mount McKinley's flanks. New life bursts onto the landscape with urgency in late May as long daylight hours bathe Denali with warmer temperatures. Moose, caribou,

"THE MOVEMENT OF THINGS ON THIS EARTH HAS ALWAYS IMPRESSED ME. THERE IS A REASSURING VITALITY IN THE ANNUAL RISE OF A RIVER, IN THE RETURN OF THE ARCTIC SUN, IN THE POLEWARD FLIGHT OF SPRING MIGRATIONS, IN THE SEASONAL TREK OF NOMADIC PEOPLES."

—John Haines, *Living Off the Country: Essays on Poetry and Place*

Shifting seasons of Denali

▼ Caribou calves can walk one hour after birth, and sprint with their herd just a day or two later. Even when they are not actively migrating, caribou travel vast distances to browse and to keep ahead of the biting flies that plague them. Occasionally, they'll seek rest and refuge atop a breezy ridge or in a cool snowfield.

sheep, and other animals that mated in fall and nurtured new life internally through icy months give birth to their young. The spindly legged creatures quickly struggle to their feet. They must be able to follow their mothers, to flee bears who have emerged hungry from winter dens and wolves who are feeding their own new young.

Herbivores of all kinds spend the summer ceaselessly grazing. Young moose will gain three to five pounds a day. Only one moose calf in ten will survive its first year. New predators must quickly learn the challenges of getting a meal; many of them will also die due to a lack of food or other hazards of life in the wild.

Autumn may be the briefest season of all, but it passes in a blaze. Nature's loom goes into overdrive. Seemingly overnight, the emerald-green tundra turns saffron, cinnamon, and russet. Fall is a time for mating. In one of the most dramatic rituals, bull moose challenge each other with large antlers they have grown all summer; they drop the antlers after the mating season.

A few months later, in midwinter, the sun will stay hidden for all but four hours each day, and temperatures may drop to forty or fifty degrees below zero. But even when it's brutally cold outside, and some of Denali's animals have migrated or are hibernating, others—such as the chickadee, the ptarmigan, and the wolf—will be as awake and busy as ever, their restlessness necessary for survival.

"Seasons tend to blow open and shut like

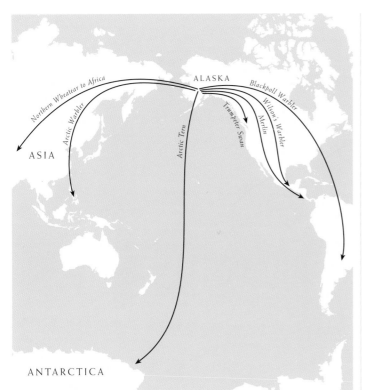

ALASKA

Northern Wheatear to Africa

Arctic Warbler

ASIA

Arctic Tern

Trumpeter Swan

Merlin

Wilson's Warbler

Blackpoll Warbler

ANTARCTICA

◄ Arctic terns (top), merlins, and trumpeter swans (bottom) are among the many species of birds that migrate to Denali in summer from thousands of miles outside Alaska. Many songbirds are attracted by good nesting habitat and abundant insects—including mosquitoes—that provide protein necessary for their reproduction.

_____

_____

_____

_____

_____

doors in the wind up here." —Aaron Coons.

► Bears may slumber all winter, but in summer they are busy consuming calories. Scientists call this manic urge to eat "hyperphagia." In a single day, the primarily vegetarian grizzly can eat 200,000 soapberries.

Many species of birds migrate to Denali in

◄ Willow ptarmigan, the state bird, can keep its body temperature at 104 degrees even when temperatures drop to nearly thirty below zero. Insulation is the key. In winter (left), it grows feathers that cover its legs and feet. As summer comes, its plumage (bottom left) changes.

▲ Golden eagles soar here. This migratory raptor preys on many animals in the park, including ground squirrels, marmots, ptarmigan, hares, and even young Dall sheep.

▼ The chickadee, a year-round resident that weighs barely half an ounce, will gorge on cached seeds to maintain its weight, and therefore its insulation. In a single day of bingeing, a chickadee can gain up to 10 percent of its body mass; that's like a 140-pound person gaining 14 pounds in one day.

summer from thousands of miles outside Alaska.

► It seems that arctic ground squirrels spend their lives in a state of perpetual anxiety, searching for food or seeking shelter from predators. The ground squirrel is eaten by wolf, lynx, fox, and wolverine. It is a main food of golden eagles and a treat for grizzly bears, which paw holes in the tundra while pursuing their favorite high-protein snack. Only in winter can the ground squirrel really rest. A true hibernator, its entire metabolism slows to a near stop; in one minute its heart may beat fewer than 10 times and it may breathe just three times.

Few mammals are as important to the

◄ A red fox carries ground squirrels home for dinner.

_____
_____
_____
_____
_____
_____
_____
_____
_____
_____

ecology of the park as the arctic ground squirrel.

Reflections

In 1972 most private Denali traffic was restricted west of Savage River. By seeing this national park by bus, from a narrow ribbon of road, you are taking part in a history-making effort to limit disturbances to a fragile landscape.

"WE SIMPLY NEED THAT WILD COUNTRY AVAILABLE TO US, EVEN IF WE NEVER DO MORE THAN DRIVE TO ITS EDGE AND LOOK IN. FOR IT CAN BE A MEANS OF REASSURING OURSELVES OF OUR SANITY AS CREATURES, A PART OF THE GEOGRAPHY OF HOPE."

—Wallace Stegner, in a letter to *Outdoor Recreation Resources Review,* 1960

A place for reflection and inspiration

"NATIONAL PARKS ARE PARADOXICAL PLACES, THEY OFFER US FREEDOM, YET REQUIRE RESTRAINT. THEY ARE BEST EXPLORED DEEPLY, YET LIGHTLY. THEY DEMAND NEW SENSIBILITIES IF WE ARE TO LEAVE THEM AS WE FOUND THEM, UNIMPAIRED. . . ."

—Kim Heacox,
National Parks
Magazine, 1999

Even after you go home, you will continue to make choices that affect Denali. Alaska may seem distant and pristine, but no place on earth is exempt from the problems of air pollution, environmental contamination, and global warming that affect us all. Nor is the weaving of any natural place ever complete. From within the park, or from thousands of miles away, we all decide whether or not the most beautiful parts of nature's designs will become unraveled.

We can choose to be like Charles Sheldon, the park's forefather. After his second visit to Alaska, Charles Sheldon did not return. Yet the spirit of Denali stayed with him. It moved him not only to reflect and remember, but also to act. By lobbying Congress, and persevering until the park became a reality, Sheldon wove his own ideals and life story into the living tapestry of Denali.

Sheldon's task was to create a national park. Our task is to maintain, defend, and preserve it—not only for our children, but also for our children's children. Some day they, too, may ride along the 91-mile ribbon of Denali's park road, and see with their own eyes that the intricate weave of wilderness still holds.

◄ Leaving the park unimpaired means new generations of

those who now live in Denali can continue to call it home.

Preserving the intricate weave of true wilderness

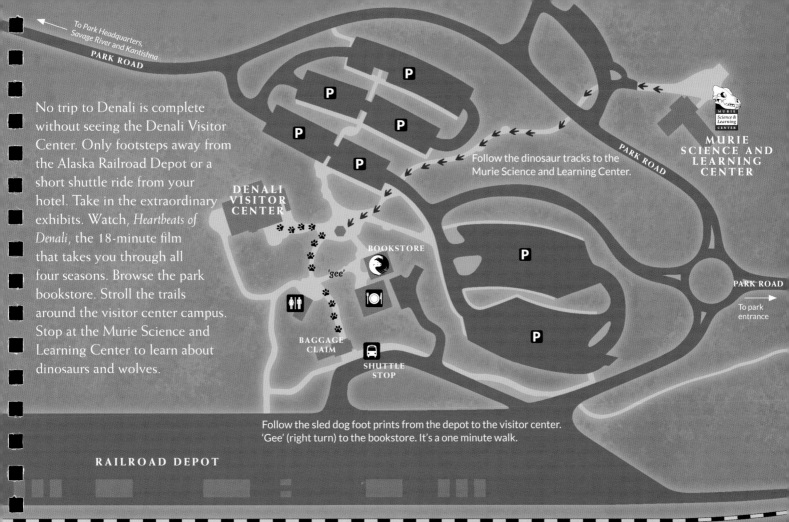

No trip to Denali is complete without seeing the Denali Visitor Center. Only footsteps away from the Alaska Railroad Depot or a short shuttle ride from your hotel. Take in the extraordinary exhibits. Watch, *Heartbeats of Denali*, the 18-minute film that takes you through all four seasons. Browse the park bookstore. Stroll the trails around the visitor center campus. Stop at the Murie Science and Learning Center to learn about dinosaurs and wolves.

To Park Headquarters, Savage River and Kantishna

PARK ROAD

PARK ROAD

MURIE SCIENCE AND LEARNING CENTER

Follow the dinosaur tracks to the Murie Science and Learning Center.

DENALI VISITOR CENTER

'gee'

BOOKSTORE

PARK ROAD

To park entrance

BAGGAGE CLAIM

SHUTTLE STOP

Follow the sled dog foot prints from the depot to the visitor center. 'Gee' (right turn) to the bookstore. It's a one minute walk.

RAILROAD DEPOT

COUPON

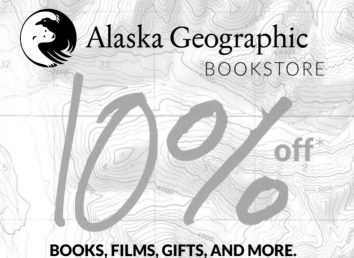

Alaska Geographic
BOOKSTORE

10% off*

BOOKS, FILMS, GIFTS, AND MORE.

Denali Visitor Center
As an easy walk from the train depot is rewarded with extraordinary exhibits, the award-winning film, *Heartbeats of Denali*, or chatting with a park ranger.

Murie Science and Learning Center
From the visitor center follow dinosaur tracks along a paved trail to experience the science based exhibits including a fully articulated wolf skeleton, animal pelts and real dinosaur tracks.

Alaska Geographic Bookstore
Stop in and use your coupon on books, films, gifts, and more. From informative to memorable, you are sure to find the right treasures to take home from your Denali experience.

Alaska Geographic

Connecting people to Alaska's wildlands